PIONEERS OF LGBTQ+ RIGHTS

THE HISTORY OF THE LGBTQ+ RIGHTS MOVEMENT™

PIONEERS OF LGBTQ+ RIGHTS

ELLEN MCGRODY

Rosen
YA™
New York

To Chris, for showing me the way; to Bradley, for giving me the strength; and to Jae, for believing I could do it. May the people in this book inspire you to keep fighting.

Published in 2019 by The Rosen Publishing Group, Inc.
29 East 21st Street, New York, NY 10010

First Edition

Library of Congress Cataloging-in-Publication Data

Names: McGrody, Ellen, author.
Title: Pioneers of LGBTQ+ rights / Ellen McGrody.
Description: New York, NY: Rosen Publishing, 2019. | Series: The history of the LGBTQ+ rights movement | Includes bibliographical references and index. | Audience: Grades 7–12.
Identifiers: LCCN 2017020371 | ISBN 9781538381304 (library bound) | 9781508183099 (pbk.)
Subjects: LCSH: Gay rights—United States—History—Juvenile literature. | Gays—United States—History—Juvenile literature.
Classification: LCC HQ76.8.U5 M395 2018 | DDC 323.3/2640973—dc23
LC record available at https://lccn.loc.gov/2017020371

Manufactured in the United States of America

On the cover: Shown here are tennis player Renée Richards (*top*) and novelist James Baldwin (*bottom*).

CONTENTS

INTRODUCTION

One common strand in progressive social movements is that oppressed people gain more rights when pioneers tirelessly lead the fight. The movement for civil rights continues to shape itself according to the needs of those seeking freedom, opportunity, and happiness. Mass movements are the vehicles of modern and contemporary progress, and pioneers are the ones who steer those vehicles.

LGBTQ+ people, in particular, have had a difficult movement to lead. They have often faced rigid social norms and sentiments that led people to deny them their rights, their dignity, and even their personhood. This kind of oppression has wreaked havoc in the lives of people of color, the poor, and those whose sexuality and gender don't match a specific kind of expression. What people from all these groups have in common is a lack of power. It is that lack of power and voice that can make the needs of oppressed groups easy to ignore for those in positions of power.

Even worse, those in power actively attempt to erase the existence of oppressed peoples. The idea that LGBTQ+ people are an invention of the twentieth century ignores the rich history of those who came before. Ancient societies, as well as some non-Western ones, have had a more mixed reception toward nonnormative sexualities and gender identities. Various indigenous peoples of the United States carved out a role for them while some weren't so accepting. Ancient Pakistani

UPTOWN TENDERLOIN
Lost Landmarks
COMPTON'S CAFETERIA RIOT
1966

ONE AUGUST EVENING IN 1966, TRANSGENDER WOMEN AND GAY MEN BANDED TOGETHER TO FIGHT BACK AGAINST OPPRESSION AFTER A POLICE OFFICER HARASSED ONE OF THEM AT GENE COMPTON'S CAFETERIA. THIS CONFRONTATION WAS THE FIRST KNOWN FULL-SCALE RIOT FOR TRANSGENDER AND GAY RIGHTS IN U.S. HISTORY. IT GALVANIZED THE COMMUNITY, PROMPTING NEW PUBLIC POLICIES AND SOCIAL SERVICES THAT IMPROVED THE LIVES OF LOCAL TRANSGENDER PEOPLE.

UPTOWN TENDERLOIN HISTORIC DISTRICT

This plaque commemorates the 1966 Compton's Cafeteria riot that occurred in San Francisco's Tenderloin District. It is located at the restaurant's former location.

and Indian cultures embraced *hijras* and *sadhins*. And Polynesian culture acknowledges various transgender identities, including *fa'fafines*, *fakaleitis*, and *mahus*.

Unlike the various transgender and nonstraight communities of many precolonial cultures, lesbians, gay men, bisexuals, transgender individuals, and all the other unique experiences and identities that fit under what's now referred to as the queer umbrella have more often been harmed by discrimination and prejudice in the colonial and postcolonial worlds. But modern and current LGBTQ+ history isn't only about the distress that has been inflicted upon them. Many queer people, inspired by the lives of those before them, have stood up to fight for their rights, and they won great progress for their efforts.

While the geographic scope of the movement for LGBTQ+ rights is international, it is impossible to offer a succinct treatment of movements that have such different implications in different countries. All discussed pioneers in this resource will include those active in the United States or those who had a particularly strong influence in the United States.

The overarching theme is that all these brave pioneers have worked toward one end: that all people, of all sexualities and genders, should be respected for who they are and can love whom they want without fear. When that end will be achieved is still unclear.

CHAPTER ONE

QUEER PIONEERS EMERGE

· ·

W estern societies snuffed out diverse ideas and expressions of gender and sexuality in the populations of the places they colonized and within their own ranks. Religion, government, and law evolved together to oppress those who weren't heterosexual, but indigenous and Eastern cultures resisted this intolerance and maintained diverse acceptance of various sexualities and gender expressions long into the nineteenth century.

This trend of suppression wouldn't dominate forever, though. As the Industrial Revolution rolled in, a larger movement to support the rights and dignity of LGBTQ+ people throughout the world began to emerge. The late nineteenth century and early twentieth century supplied fertile ground for advocates of gay rights. Early organizers established the first societies for equality, bravely rallied their governments to reconsider antigay laws, and began compiling the knowledge and language that would guide the movement into the future.

The twentieth century also brought on changes. Even in the face of fascism's rise during World War II, some of the first homosexual advocacy groups appeared, along with the earliest medical treatments for those who were then referred to as transsexuals. The terminology and definitions used to express the breadth of human sexualities and gender expressions began to appear during these years, first by the organizations that worked to bring these people together under a common umbrella and then by the general population.

EMMA GOLDMAN

American anarcho-communist Emma Goldman was considered by European gay rights activists to be "the most adamant ally of sexual inverts in North America." Goldman was born in 1869 in Lithuania before emigrating to the United States in 1885. She moved to Rochester, New York, and began working as a seamstress.

In the conditions of a clothing factory, she began to sympathize with the plight of her fellow workers and began studying anarchist and communist thought. She became a writer and wrote on topics concerning birth control, emancipation, universal suffrage, and an end to the draft. She wrote books like *Anarchism and Other Essays* and wrote for popular magazines like *Mother Earth*. Meanwhile, she was also busy inciting factory strikes and engaging in an international lecture circuit. It was

In 1916, Emma Goldman rouses a crowd with a speech in New York City's Union Square. She is urging direct action for workers' and women's rights.

in those lecture circuits that Goldman learned of a growing gay rights movement and began incorporating its ideas in her own writing.

Goldman's writing introduced a growing socialist left in the United States to the cause of gay rights. Queer history buff Sadie Ryanne recalls a 1923 letter to Magnus Hirschfeld, founder of the Institute for Sex Research, in which Goldman wrote, "It is a tragedy, I feel, that people of a different sexual type are caught in a world which shows so little understanding for homosexuals, is so crassly indifferent to the various gradations and variations of gender and their great significance in life." In fact, her fight for the rights of all people, particularly women, included a staunch platform for the legalization of homosexuality. This level of progressivism was unheard of even in the most radical of circles during her time.

Goldman remained a staunch leftist until the end of her life. She was arrested several times in the United States under laws like the Comstock Law, which deemed several kinds of literature to be obscene, and the Espionage Act, under which she was imprisoned for encouraging people not to register for the World War I draft. Shortly afterwards, she was deported under the Anarchist Exclusion Act, and her international travels found her struggling to find a voice amidst the Great Depression. She remained adamantly against war as World War II seemed imminent and passed away in Toronto in 1940, shortly after the war began.

GENDER AND SEXUALITY IN EARLY AMERICA

The religious settlers who governed the American colonies often passed laws that made homosexuality illegal. Author Rachel Hope Cleves wrote about two queer women in early nineteenth century Vermont named Sylvia Drake and Charity Bryant who weren't prosecuted under these laws. They lived together for over forty years in a relationship that was a marital one in spirit, although not in name.

Cleves described their experience by writing, "Charity and Sylvia gained the toleration of their relatives and community not by hiding away but by being public-minded." They loved each other deeply and depended on each other, as would any other married couple. They were known in their small country town as Aunt Sylvia and Aunt Charity and served as community leaders. Clearly, not all colonists were eager to enforce conformity.

The Native American cultures that were contemporary to Drake and Bryant and precolonial ones shared a rich tradition of gender and sexual expression that differed vastly from colonists' views. Born into a Zuni tribe in 1849, We'wha was a Native American from New Mexico whom author Will Roscoe wrote about in *The Zuni Man-Woman*. We'wha was a *lhamana*, a traditional Zuni gender role under which those assigned male at birth performed the roles traditionally held by women and wore the garb

(continued on the next page)

(continued from the previous page)

traditionally worn by women. This kind of gender role existed in many Native American societies. In fact, mixed-gender or two-spirit identities were prevalent in various indigenous cultures.

We'wha is known for having met President Grover Cleveland at the White House during a visit sponsored by anthropologist Matilda Coxe Stephenson. We'wha was presumed to be a woman, so We'wha faced no objections to performing a gender role that generally wasn't accepted in American society. Whether on purpose or accidentally, Drake, Bryant, and We'wha weren't harmed by any laws or stigma.

MAGNUS HIRSCHFELD

German physician Magnus Hirschfeld dedicated himself to studying and advocating for his peers. Upon beginning his career in medicine, Hirschfeld was immediately drawn to the study of human sexuality and gender. Hirschfeld believed that sexual orientation and gender identity were natural and inherent traits worthy of scientific study and social liberation. He wrote and worked under his given name, a revolutionary act at the time for those who studied such subjects, and encouraged others to do the same.

Hirschfeld identified as a homosexual man and as a transvestite, a term he coined to refer to those

Magnus Hirschfeld was a self-identified homosexual man and cross-dresser who pioneered scientific research on LGBTQ+ individuals. He founded the Institute for Sex Research in Berlin in 1919.

who engaged in cross-dressing, or dressing in clothing traditionally worn by those of the opposing gender (in a gender binary). His own personal leanings and the bravery of those around him inspired him to become a sexologist and to dedicate his career to creating vital societies for the betterment of LGBTQ+ people.

In 1897, Hirschfeld founded the Scientific Humanitarian Committee (Wissenschaftlich-humanitäres Komitee), the world's first public organization for LGBTQ+ rights. As a renowned speaker and sexologist, he worked with more than thirty thousand men and women to help them live more honest lives. Driven by the cause to study sexuality and fight for

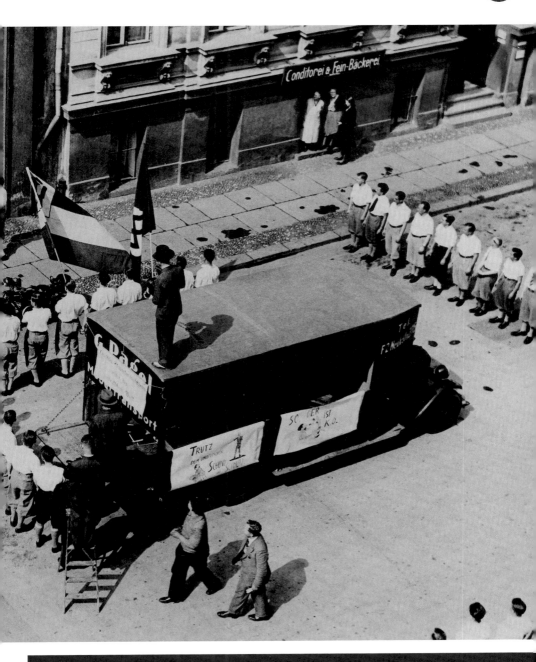

Members of the Hitler Youth movement demonstrate here outside of the Institute for Sex Research on May 6, 1933, days before the Nazi government raided the institute and burned its literary collection.

legal welfare, Hirschfeld also founded the Institute for Sex Research (Institut für Sexualwissenschaft) in 1919. The institute provided therapeutic treatment for "sexual inversion," a Victorian-era term referring to gender-variant and sexually diverse individuals.

Hirschfeld's institute was responsible for the first medical gender transition options. Its research was utilized to provide hormonal and surgical treatment options to transgender people. The institute also fought hard to eradicate sexual-deviancy laws throughout the world.

Hirschfeld's early actions were instrumental in normalizing homosexuality and transsexuality and to bringing the gay rights movement into North America. The same year the institute was founded, Hirschfeld produced *Different from the Others*, a documentary showcasing his therapeutic treatment of LGBTQ+ people. The film was released across Europe and North America and was hugely influential.

The ongoing struggle for gay rights in Germany suffered great damage due to the Great Depression and the rise of fascism. While Hirschfeld continued working after World War I, his ultimate struggle to decriminalize homosexuality in Germany ended with the rise of the Nazis.

Hirschfeld left Germany in 1930 for a book tour just after the economy crashed. This was before the Nazis took power in 1933. Shortly before Hirschfeld's death in 1935, the Nazis burned down the library of work at the institute, and many of

Hirschfeld's LGBTQ+ peers became victims of the Holocaust. Many of Hirschfeld's books and films have survived, however, and his work forever changed the landscape of LGBTQ+ rights.

HENRY GERBER

Following in the footsteps of Hirschfeld, Henry Gerber attempted to create a political structure for homosexual rights in the United States as early as 1924. Henry Gerber was born in Germany and lived in Bavaria until his family moved to Chicago in 1913. In Chicago, Gerber found himself victimized by antihomosexual laws when he was briefly committed to a mental institution. Upon the breakout of World War I, he was forced by immigration policy to become a soldier. It was as an American soldier in Germany that he learned of Magnus Hirschfeld's institute and became inspired to attempt to create a similar organization at home.

Gerber attempted to create several groups that were blocked by the political tides in the United States. When he came back to Chicago in 1924, he created the Society for Human Rights, the first gay rights organization in the United States. The distribution of the society's publication, *Friendship and Freedom*, went against the Comstock Act, which deemed all progay publications to be obscene. The society came to an unfortunate end when the daughter of a closeted member reported it

Anthony Comstock was a postal inspector who founded the New York Society for the Suppression of Vice. That society advocated for laws permitting censorship of literature and conduct it deemed obscene or pornographic.

to social workers, prompting the state to arrest several of its members.

After the failure of the Society for Human Rights, Gerber did not stop advocating for homosexual rights. He continued to write progay pieces and distribute gay-advocacy publications, often under the pen name Parisex. He submitted pieces to *The Modern Thinker*, the *Mattachine Review*, and *ONE*. He passed away at eighty years old in 1972. In 1992, Gerber was inducted into the Chicago Gay and Lesbian Hall of Fame, and his house in the city was declared a National Historic Landmark.

CHAPTER TWO

COMING TOGETHER AFTER THE WAR

• •

While World War II damaged some of the emerging organizations for gay equality, the war directly influenced the trajectory of the coming movement. Soldiers came back from the war and found partners and lived their lives as fully as they could. For straight people, this led to the postwar baby boom. This period also gave way to a mass civil rights movement by people of color during the late 1950s and the 1960s. For LGBTQ+ people, the postwar period was a time in which many of them admitted their identities for the first time. It meant starting groups, finding partners, or taking advantage of gender-affirming surgeries.

For some, the goal of these early decades of organization was blending in with society at large. This was reflected in the push toward mainstream recognition of gay issues in both science and politics. For others, being gay was something to be celebrated and treated as unique and special. This discourse kindled productive and forward-thinking conversations in gay clubs and later in the pages of

LGBTQ+ publications. These communities brought people together and prepared them to fight for recognition, as there always seemed to be some battle to wage.

EDYTHE EYDE

One of the earliest prominent authors of a gay-interest publication was Los Angeles's Edythe Eyde. She was born in San Francisco in 1921. Eyde developed an antagonistic relationship with her parents and peers because of her unique and sometimes abrasive personality. As a child, she developed a crush and had a brief relationship with another girl. That relationship ended poorly, and she moved through life focusing on school and work.

She took a secretarial course and became an administrative assistant at RKO Studio. It was then, living in an apartment in Los Angeles, that she realized she was gay. She frequented Los Angeles gay bars and began writing an advocacy and culture magazine for lesbian women during slow hours at RKO in 1947. This magazine, *Vice Versa*, became the first lesbian periodical. It was passed around by Eyde from friend to friend and eventually became a stalwart publication in the Southern California gay scene.

Eyde later joined one of the first lesbian advocacy groups, the Daughters of Bilitis. She wrote for their magazine, *The Ladder*, under the pen name Lisa Ben, an anagram of the word "lesbian." She wrote about gay life and sang folk songs about being a gay woman. Those songs had titles like "I'm Gonna Sit Down and Write My Butch a Letter" and "The Vice Squad Keeps Breaking Up That Old Gang of Mine." Her songs and writing reflected a burgeoning gay culture and were rich with the concerns and experiences of gay men and women throughout America.

She died in 2015. She is remembered as someone who expressed "unapologetic enthusiasm" for connecting people and telling stories.

EDWARD SAGARIN GIVES DONALD WEBSTER CORY A VOICE

Gay author Edward Sagarin (September 18, 1913– June 10, 1986) took his pen name, Donald Webster Cory, from a gay character that French author André Gide created.

Living in New York, Sagarin lived a troublesome double life. By day, as Sagarin, he was married with a child and worked as a college professor and a scientist. He published a book on perfumery.

But as Donald Webster Cory, he wrote a bombshell of a book—*The Homosexual in America*. "One great gap separates the homosexual minority from all others," Sagarin

Senator Joseph McCarthy (R-WI) publicly alleged that there were large numbers of Communists and Soviet spies in the federal government.

wrote, "and that is its lack of recognition, its lack of respectability in the eyes of the public, and even in the most advanced circles." Sagarin's words offered a bitter, revolutionary truth to the gay men and women who read his work. His book detailed the treatment of gays and lesbians throughout American society and described the impact of policies that marginalized gay people.

Marginalizing gay people was a particularly high priority of the US government during the lavender scare. During this period of the early 1950s, Senator Joseph McCarthy led the charge to rid the government of any homosexual civil servant. Sagarin's work was also relatable to those who received a blue discharge, a somewhat neutral military discharge that left recipients (many of whom were gay) barred from receiving any veterans' benefits. Sagarin wrote with an empowered and rattled voice, a voice for those who cried out for dignity and respect in a cruel time.

Sagarin continued to write other books on gay theory as Cory, including studies focused specifically on lesbians. Though he later came to disagree with parts of the ongoing LGBTQ+ rights movement in the 1970s, Sagarin continued to advocate for gay liberation until he was forced to withdraw from the movement when his true identity was exposed at a conference in 1974. He passed away from a heart attack at his home in New York in 1986.

ALFRED KINSEY

Alfred Kinsey was born in New Jersey in 1894. A devout Methodist upbringing left him detached from sexuality and romantic expression, but he somehow came to be fascinated with biology and human sexuality. He began his work at Indiana University as a professor of marital study in 1920.

Kinsey started his surveys on sexuality in 1938, and in the midst of this research, he incorporated the Institute for Sex Research (currently known as the Kinsey Institute) in 1947. These surveys led him to twenty-five years of interviewing nearly twenty thousand men and women about their sexual preferences and habits. He asked questions about topics like masturbation, sexual intercourse, and homosexuality. Kinsey's studies led to the publication of two pioneering books, *Sexual Behavior in the Human Male* and *Sexual Behavior in the Human Female*.

The statistics revealed by the research in his books were shocking at the time. Kinsey's studies illustrated an America that wasn't as puritanical as it liked to portray itself, and during the time of the lavender scare, the idea that a vast chunk of the US populace had participated in sexually diverse experiences was shocking. At the same time, his research sought to normalize homosexuality, bisexuality, and asexuality by

Alfred Kinsey speaks to a large crowd at the University of California, Berkeley in 1949. He is discussing his findings concerning sexual behavior in women.

portraying them as common and natural parts of the human condition. Additionally, Kinsey's books introduced the Kinsey Scale of Sexuality, a flawed but revolutionary method of portraying sexuality as a spectrum with many different options and variations. This six-point scale is relatively simple. According to the Kinsey Institute, "People at '0' report exclusively heterosexual/opposite sex behavior or attraction. Those at '6' report exclusively homosexual/same-sex behavior or attraction." Ratings 1 to 5 represent different variations of bisexuality, and an X represented asexuality. This scale set the foundation for a normalization and expansion of exploration regarding sexual orientation and gender identity.

Kinsey's work was unlike anything else done at the time. His books would go on to inspire later activists to form gay rights organizations and bring the movement forward. But he was not without controversy. Later scholars criticized some of his methodology. Some accused him of mistreating and abusing his subjects and not disclosing information about at least one sexual predator he studied. But even if done again now using more currently acceptable methods, it would be clear that Kinsey's work would do much to humanize a previously demonized part of existence.

EVELYN HOOKER

Evelyn Hooker was born in 1907. She spent most of her youth with her mother and siblings in Sterling, Colorado. She studied psychology at the University of Colorado before earning her doctorate at Johns Hopkins University. As a psychology teacher, she befriended a gay student, Sam From, at the University of California, Los Angeles. Her friendship with From inspired her to do more research on homosexual men, including surveys she conducted throughout the late 1940s and early 1950s. She eventually sought to challenge the doctrine of homosexuality as a mental health disorder.

The *Diagnostic and Statistical Manual of Mental Disorders* has a tumultuous history of revisions that redefined psychological disorders. The fifth edition, published in 2013, reclassified gender dysphoria in a way that was similar to revisions that resituated homosexuality.

Hooker's research earned her a grant from the National Institute for Mental Health. Using the work of Alfred Kinsey to guide her own, she aimed to study the way the brain differed between homosexual and heterosexual men. Her theory posited that if homosexuality truly was a mental disorder, it should impact the cognitive function of homosexual people. Her studies, based on standard methodology used to study cognitive function, discovered that homosexual and heterosexual brains were functionally alike. This research reflected her "long advocacy of a scientific view of homosexuality," according to the American Psychiatric Association. Her findings were instrumental in the later efforts that successfully changed and then removed homosexuality from the *Diagnostic and Statistical Manual of Mental Disorders* in 1973 and 1987, respectively.

MIDCENTURY AMERICAN TRANSGENDER LIFE

In an era in which treatment for transgender people was becoming more accessible, it became easier to find examples of transgender people living their lives with dignity throughout America. One such transgender person was Christine Jorgensen. Being drafted into the military during World War II only amplified her gender dysphoria, and upon her return to the United States, she began taking female hormones on her own based on literature she found. She then went to Sweden, the first country in the world to legalize gender transition. She ended up in Denmark, where surgeon Christian Hamburger agreed to put Jorgensen on a stricter regimen of hormone replacement therapy and prepare her for surgery.

A *New York Daily News* headline that read "Ex-GI Becomes Blonde Beauty!" gave Jorgensen instant worldwide celebrity for undergoing gender transition surgery. While she faced discrimination from those who didn't quite understand her condition, she lived her life with grace, becoming a nightclub singer and endeavoring to cross the country in a lecture circuit on transgender issues.

Most transgender people at the time, however, didn't have access to the medical treatment that Jorgensen sought in Denmark. Billy Tipton was one such man. Tipton was known to America as the leader of the Billy Tipton Trio, a moderately successful jazz outfit. Tipton was a talented musician who was skilled in playing both the piano and the saxophone.

Although he lived as a man, Tipton was assigned female at birth and was what would be considered now a straight transgender man. This truth came to light only upon his death.

Tipton and Jorgensen stand as early examples of how transgender people began to find their place in society at large.

HARRY HAY

One of the first successful queer organizers, Harry Hay was a Communist Party member who spent much of his youth participating in labor organizations and cultural work.

Hay was born in 1912 in England and spent part of his childhood there before his family moved to Los Angeles in 1919. The abuse he received from his father and the environment of intolerance toward gays galvanized him from a young age to make safe spaces for those like him to congregate and organize.

Hay was a committed leftist organizer. He discreetly registered for the Communist Party in 1934 before McCarthyism had reached its peak. He worked in Hollywood, like many leftists, and organized

Harry Hay was eighty-four years old in this 1998 photo. He left behind a legacy of fighting for oppressed LGBTQ+ people and poor people.

workers' strikes and Communist actions under the cover of darkness. Believing that legislation was the only way forward for gay equality, Hay began campaigning for progressive candidate and former vice president Henry A. Wallace when Wallace ran for president in 1948. He pledged the gay vote to the Progressive Party as he began drafting policy proposals that fit the needs of the burgeoning gay community. While Wallace's campaign was a failure, campaigning on Wallace's behalf allowed Hay to meet peers like Rudi Gernreich. He partnered with those peers to build an underground society for gay men called the Mattachine Society in 1950.

With the threat of McCarthyism looming over the group, Hay decided to model the Mattachine Society after left-wing cells. Working with Gernreich, the early Mattachine meetings consisted of discussion groups regarding Alfred Kinsey's studies of gay men. Mattachine blossomed into a group of more than five thousand people in California alone. The group won early legal victories that included defending Dale Jennings from police entrapment. They also began publishing the *Mattachine Review*, a formative publication for the gay movement.

As the Mattachine Society began to grow and form cells in other cities throughout the country, its members began to advocate more for blending in with heterosexual society. Seeing that the desires of most members began to stray from his own leftist vision, Hay left the group on unfriendly terms. Hay laid low in the gay rights movement for a while after that. He met his future life partner, the inventor John Burnside, at a meeting of the Mattachine spin-off group called ONE. Some time after that, he returned to a resurgent leftist gay movement in the 1970s.

He later served as the grand marshal of the San Francisco Lesbian, Gay, Bisexual, Transgender Pride Parade in 1999. He passed away in San Francisco in 2002 at ninety years old with Burnside by his side.

PHYLLIS LYON AND DEL MARTIN

The stories of Phyllis Lyon and Del Martin are intertwined. Martin, born Dorothy Louise Taliaferro, was born in San Francisco in 1921. She graduated from high school and college with honors and resolved to pursue a career in journalism. Lyon, born in 1924 in Oklahoma, was also a journalism student. She moved to California to pursue college and again to Seattle to work as a magazine editor.

Martin and Lyon met in Seattle. They formed a strong bond and became partners in 1953. They then moved to San Francisco and explored the city's growing gay scene and its many lesbian bars.

Even among the bars and cafes that housed gay culture at the time, Lyon and Martin found the sense of unity among lesbians to be unsatisfactory. In an interview cited by San Francisco history archive FoundSF, Martin elaborates: "It was like there were places to go for entertainment and there was a certain ambience, but there was not the sense of community that we have developed since."

Phyllis Lyon (*left*) and Del Martin (*right*) are shown here at their wedding reception in San Francisco on February 22, 2014.

As the Mattachine Society and ONE began to create cells across the country, many gay and lesbian individuals were gathering in secret social clubs to discuss their needs. Martin and Lyon were invited to one such meeting in 1955. The result of this meeting was that they founded a new society, the Daughters of Bilitis. They chose to name it after a poetry collection depicting a lesbian woman in ancient Greece by author Pierre Louys.

The Daughters of Bilitis quickly gained popularity among lesbians in San Francisco. It served as a lesbian analogue to the Mattachine Society, providing women with a way to congregate socially in safety and secrecy.

The Daughters of Bilitis partnered with other homophile organizations to combat oppression against the queer community and normalize its presence in society at large. Martin became the group's first president and Lyon became the first editor of its publication, *The Ladder*. *The Ladder* housed the work of writers such as Broadway playwright Lorraine Hansberry and influential lesbian author Edythe Eyde. Lyon and Martin also wrote contributions ranging from short stories to condemnations of sexism in the larger gay movement for *The Ladder*.

The Daughters of Bilitis published the last issue of *The Ladder* in 1972 before dissolving, and Lyon and Martin stepped away in pursuit of further activism. Martin worked with the Council on Religion and the Homosexual to create policy proposals that would reduce police harassment and legalize gay relationships. The couple joined the ranks of the National Organization for Women, a leading feminist activism group. There, Martin joined the board as NOW's first lesbian director. The two continued to fight for both lesbian equality and women's rights as a whole. They also founded shelters for victims of domestic violence and gay political clubs, such as the influential Alice B. Toklas LGBT Democratic Club.

Lyon and Martin received recognition from the American Civil Liberties Union (ACLU), the Society for the Scientific Study of Sexuality, *Publishers Weekly*, and other organizations. Local health providers in the Bay Area further honored their dedication by naming a women and LGBT-focused health clinic in their honor, a clinic which continues to provide health care to marginalized people throughout Northern California.

Lyon and Martin's partnership was long and full. They were the first couple to marry when gay marriage became legal in San Francisco under Mayor Gavin Newsom in 2004 and married again in 2008 after the California Supreme Court reaffirmed the right for same-sex couples to marry. Del Martin passed away shortly after their second marriage, while Phyllis Lyon continued to provide inspiration and a guiding light for lesbian women and LGBTQ+ people everywhere.

CHAPTER THREE

A CIVIL RIGHTS REVOLUTION

T he 1960s and 1970s were a tumultuous time for the fight for human rights. Empowered by the societies and science laid down in the 1950s and inspired by people of color leading protests and nonviolent action, LGBTQ+ people began to stand up and stand out. What ensued led to LGBTQ+ people and their needs becoming more visible in politics and popular culture.

JAMES BALDWIN

African American author James Baldwin was a pivotal voice in the civil rights movement. By the time the movement took off, Baldwin was already a successful and prolific writer because he had published two incredibly influential books during the 1950s. His writing throughout the 1960s and 1970s would shape cultural perceptions regarding black issues and same-sex relationships.

James Baldwin, the grandson of a slave, was born in 1924 in Harlem, in New York City. He was the oldest of nine children raised in a traditionally

James Baldwin is shown here in a hotel in Montgomery, Alabama, in March 1965. On this trip, he was participating in the Student Nonviolent Coordinating Committee march from Selma to Montgomery with the purpose of advocating for equal voting rights.

religious family. His stepfather was a preacher, and while they had a tumultuous relationship, Baldwin followed in his footsteps and immersed himself in the language of the Bible as a teenager. He found refuge in the act of writing and in literature, but his religious upbringing influenced much of his later work.

At the age of eighteen, he became a railroad worker in New Jersey. He traveled via train while writing book reviews and other freelance pieces. During a short time in New York, fellow African American novelist Richard Wright helped him secure a writing grant. Baldwin used it to move to Paris and write his first novel, *Go Tell It on the Mountain* (1953). He moved to Istanbul and eventually returned to New York. Some works he completed during this time were the well-received essay collections *Notes of a Native Son* and *Nobody Knows My Name* and the novels *Another Country* and *Giovanni's Room*.

INTERSECTIONS IN THE CIVIL RIGHTS MOVEMENT

The civil rights movement fought against segregation and discrimination. It achieved many hard-earned victories throughout the 1960s and 1970s. There were several key people in that fight. In April 1960, Ella Baker, an African American student at Shaw University, founded the Student Nonviolent Coordinating

Committee (SNCC). This group acted as one of the foremost players in the movement for desegregation and equality for African Americans. Under the stewardship of leadership organizations like SNCC, Martin Luther King Jr.'s Southern Christian Leadership Conference (SCLC), and others, people of color organized to fight for desegregation in American society through protest and action.

Of course, there were LGBTQ+ people of color within the civil rights movement whose advocacy was for multiple demographics. In addition to James Baldwin, LGBTQ+ people within the civil rights movement included Lorraine Hansberry, a Broadway playwright whose work includes pieces in *The Ladder* and the play *A Raisin in the Sun*; Bayard Rustin, who advocated that Martin Luther King Jr. utilize nonviolent protest before organizing the 1963 March on Washington; and Pauli Murray, a lawyer who advocated for lesbian rights while fighting Jim Crow laws targeting black people and what she came to call Jane Crow laws, those discriminating against women.

In 1964, President Lyndon Johnson signed the Civil Rights Act into law, following it with the Voting Rights Act in 1965. These acts worked to end segregation in employment, housing, voter registration, and public places. Its passage inspired the Education Amendments of 1972, or the Patsy Mink Equal Opportunity in Education Act, which decreed that no person in the United States shall be discriminated against in education on the basis of their race or sex. These acts, and specifically Title IX of the Education Amendments, have been used to defend the rights of LGBTQ+ people up into the modern era.

Giovanni's Room earned Baldwin significant criticism for exposing a more private side of his life. It was in this novel that Baldwin first publicly explored homosexuality and bisexuality. Baldwin knew from a young age that he was gay. His sexuality impacted his relationship with religion and guided aspects of the development of *Giovanni's Room*, including themes of discovering identity and social alienation. The book tells the story of two lovers, David and Giovanni, who begin an affair in Paris. It describes the impact that hiding their relationship had on them and the people around them.

Upon returning to the United States in the late 1950s, Baldwin began touring the American South. He worked with director Elia Kazan as a playwright while learning about and participating in the burgeoning civil rights movement. It was in these travels through the South that Baldwin began work on what would become an essential piece of civil rights literature, *The Fire Next Time* (1963). He became friends with many figures in the movement, including Martin Luther King Jr. and Malcolm X. Baldwin left the country for France after their assassinations to write *If Beale Street Could Talk*.

Baldwin continued to live in St. Paul de Vence, France, for the remainder of his life. He published many other essays and continued to travel throughout the world. Baldwin lectured in California and Massachusetts and participated in an international writers' symposium in Russia. In 1987, Baldwin died of stomach cancer at his home in St. Paul de Vence, and he was celebrated by thousands at a funeral in New York.

After his death, pieces of an unpublished work, *Remember This House*, were revisited for a film by Haitian director Raoul Peck. The work described the assassinations of three of his close friends: Medgar Evers, Martin Luther King Jr., and Malcolm X. The thirty existing pages of this work were combined with archival interview footage of Baldwin in the Oscar-nominated documentary, *I Am Not Your Negro* (2016).

MARSHA P. JOHNSON

Born in New Jersey in 1945, Marsha "Pay It No Mind" Johnson was assigned male at birth but expressed gender variance from a young age. She tried on dresses at as young as five years old despite her mother's stern warning against holding a nonconforming identity.

As a young adult, Johnson broke away from her traditional, religious family. She identified as a drag queen and as a transvestite and eventually presented a feminine identity at nearly all times. Like many trans women of color, she often found herself homeless and marginalized. She also struggled with mental illness.

At twenty-five, Johnson was celebrating her birthday at a bar she frequently patronized, the Stonewall Inn. The Stonewall Inn was one of many gay bars in New York City. The conditions of its

The *Sunday News'* July 6, 1969, issue reported the events of the Stonewall riot. The headline alone has a variety of insensitive terms describing the queer patrons who resisted police brutality.

ownership and status of its liquor license, along with police prejudice toward queer individuals and cross-dressers often led to police raids on the bar. But the night of Johnson's twenty-fifth birthday wouldn't be business as usual because that night the patrons would not accept police harassment.

According to historian and Stonewall veteran David Carter, Johnson was one of the first individuals at the bar to throw glass bottles at the raiding police officers. The police were struggling to herd a bunch of patrons into a police wagon. The situation inside and outside the bar quickly dissolved into a riot that lasted for days. Johnson fought alongside many marginalized members of the community that night and in the nights that followed.

Johnson had a prominent place in the heart of the New York queer community before and after Stonewall. She was known for her colorful style and her love of the stage. She was also known for performing in local band Hot Peaches with other drag queens and gay men. After Stonewall, Johnson teamed up with a close friend, Sylvia Rivera, to found the Street Transvestite Action Revolutionaries (STAR). STAR attempted to create safe spaces for homeless and endangered transsexuals, transvestites, and drag queens, generally trans women of color. During the AIDS crisis, Johnson became an active member of AIDS Coalition to Unleash Power (ACT UP), an organization formed to protest the Reagan administration's inaction in the face of the AIDS epidemic. She lost many friends to AIDS and was diagnosed with the disease in 1990. She encouraged everyone she could to stand by those with AIDS, to treat them with the dignity and respect they deserved, and to comfort them.

Johnson passed away in 1992. Her death was ruled a suicide, but her friends believe she was murdered because her body was found in the Hudson River. Police revisited the case in 2012 and many have continued to investigate the mysterious circumstances of her untimely passing. Hundreds congregated at Johnson's preferred church in New York City for her funeral. Sylvia Rivera continued much of the work of STAR long after Johnson's death.

STONEWALL AND GAY LIBERATION

Despite previous riots that protested police brutality against the LGBTQ+ community, the Stonewall riots in 1969 were the major tipping point in the LGBTQ+ rights movement.

The Mafia had pledged to protect the Stonewall Inn, as well as other gay bars as spaces where LGBTQ+ people could congregate. In return, they could use the bars as spaces to sell drugs and extort funding. The neighborhood surrounding Stonewall, Greenwich Village in Manhattan, was a hotspot for queer people in New York. Stonewall served as a home of sorts for sex workers, butch lesbians, gender-questioning individuals, drag queens, transvestites, transsexuals, and other homeless queer youth.

In the early hours of June 28, 1969, police began a raid on Stonewall. Standard police behavior was to check all patrons in such bars for their identification cards and arrest anyone they determined was cross-dressing. Those who weren't arrested began to gather outside and heckle the cops. They soon formed a very large crowd outside the building.

The crowd began to fight the police after a butch lesbian woman was beaten while being arrested. Those remaining inside began a violent resistance against the police, with many historians arguing that Marsha P. Johnson threw the first shot glass while in the bar. The

(continued on the next page)

(continued from the previous page)

crowd and police clashed for hours before the street cleared. Violence resumed the following night and throughout the week.

Many gay organizations capitalized on the spirit of dissent by protesting around the country. Those who supported the militant revolutionary style employed at Stonewall broke away from the older groups like the Mattachine Society and created the Gay Liberation Front, a short-lived group modeled after the Black Panthers' radical action, and the Gay Activists Alliance, a more tactics-focused organization that aimed to disrupt politicians and force them to acknowledge gay rights.

lore than three thousand people marched in the second annual Gay
ride Parade in New York City. The parade was held to commemorate
hristopher Street Liberation Day on June 27, 1971.

SYLVIA RIVERA

Trans activist Sylvia Rivera was born in 1951 to a Puerto Rican father and a Venezuelan mother. She was assigned male at birth. Her father abandoned her and her mother at a very young age, and at three years old, she lost her mother to suicide. From then on, her grandmother, who disapproved of the feminine behavior she expressed from a young age, raised her. She ran away from home at the age of eleven and began making a living as a sex worker before being taken in by the New York City drag community. In the drag community, she took on the name Sylvia and began identifying as a woman.

Sylvia Rivera leads AIDS Coalition to Unleash Power (ACT UP) in the 1994 New York City Gay Pride Parade.

As a homeless queer youth in New York, she frequented the safest spaces that LGBTQ+ people had access to. Those were gay bars and cafes. Stonewall was one of these spaces, and Rivera was a frequent attendee well before the riots. Historians debate whether or not she was present at the initial police raid at Stonewall, though most agree that she participated in the riots that followed in the days after. Because she was friends with other trans women of color, especially Marsha P. Johnson, she was very closely connected to the events at Stonewall and the movement that emerged afterward. She participated in many of the meetings held by the Gay Liberation Front and the Gay Activists Alliance and advocated fiercely for gender-variant people every step of the way.

After the activities of STAR, the group she and Johnson founded slowed in the early 1970s, she oriented her work toward Pride events. Though she mourned deeply after the death of Marsha P. Johnson, she returned to STAR in 2001 and committed the rest of her life to granting transgender women of color the dignity they deserve.

Rivera passed away from liver cancer in 2002. Her legacy was carried on by activist Dean Spade, who named the Sylvia Rivera Law Project in her honor. The project was founded months after her death to provide accessible legal services to gender-variant people and continues to do so.

CHAPTER FOUR

BEYOND STONEWALL

● ●

I n the 1970s, Pride celebrations spread every
year while gay people began to demand political
action, take office, and own their identities in a
public way. Though years of hardship loomed on the
horizon, this decade was incredibly positive for the
gay rights movement.

Charged with ambition, the gay rights movement
began to splinter into several groups. Some, such
as the Gay Liberation Front, focused on more
militant actions that would fight for radical change.
Groups like these diverged from older groups,
like the Mattachine Society, because they were
more interested in pursuing fierce and proud gay
expression charged with leftist principles that
included recognition of the oppresion of people of
color and those with other marginalized identities.
Others, such as the Gay Activists Alliance and the
National Gay Task Force, focused on tactics and
worked to propel gay people into positions of power
and encourage public ownership and integration of
LGBTQ+ identities. In addition, the 1970s found
bisexual people fighting for visibility and advocacy,

Thousands of LGBTQ+ people and their allies marched on Washington on October 14, 1979, at the first National March on Washington for Lesbian and Gay Rights.

with groups such as the National Bisexual Liberation Group, the Committee of Friends of Bisexuality, and the San Francisco Bisexual Center becoming anchors in a growing part of the LGBTQ+ movement. While these groups often disagreed, their actions complemented each other to produce a range of productive outcomes for the movement.

The 1970s ended with a massive LGBTQ+ march, the National March on Washington for Gay and Lesbian Rights, on October 4, 1979. LGBTQ+ activists throughout the country came together to plan the march. They achieved a turnout of more than one hundred thousand activists. Led by the Salsa Soul Sisters, a lesbian women of color organization, the marchers came to Washington, D.C., with a list of demands for LGBTQ+ equality. The aftermath of the march, full of productive conversations with legislators, left activists optimistic about the future.

HARVEY MILK

Harvey Milk exemplified the tactical end of the gay rights movement by becoming the world's first prominent gay politician. Born in New York in 1930, his family ran a department store and founded a synagogue.

Milk studied math and history in college and wrote for the student newspaper before joining the Navy in 1951. He resigned from the Navy after being officially questioned about his

Harvey Milk served as city supervisor in San Francisco. He returned the support he received from the gay community and other marginalized people by advocating for laws that extended equality to them.

sexual orientation. He knew he was gay and wasn't willing to continue hiding his orientation.

Upon returning to civilian life, he quickly became interested in politics and activism. This led him to protest against the Vietnam War. In 1972, he moved to San Francisco and opened a camera store in the heart of the city's gay neighborhood on Castro Street. His shop quickly became a neighborhood social center. In 1973, he declared his candidacy for the San Francisco Board of Supervisors.

Though he lost that election, Milk was not deterred from his political goals. He joined forces with other Castro Street business owners to form the Castro Village Association, the first business association in the country made up of LGBTQ+ business owners. In 1975, Mayor George Moscone made Milk the first openly gay city commissioner in the United States by appointing him to the city's Board of Permit Appeals. And, after a failed bid for a seat on the state assembly, a change to San Francisco election laws ended favorably for Milk by allowing him to win a seat on the Board of Supervisors in 1978. This election, a first for the gay community, made headlines across the world.

During his tenure, he was a progressive and generally popular politician who fought for gay rights and advocated for low-cost housing, accessible family services, tax code reform, community policing, and other progressive policies on behalf of vulnerable people and families.

Milk campaigned against state policies that would harm LGBTQ+ people. He vigorously opposed the Briggs Initiative, a proposed mandate to fire gay teachers and sympathizers of the gay community in California schools. He also advocated for workers and participated in the San Francisco Pride Parade in 1978.

At the end of November that year, former city supervisor Dan White assassinated both Harvey Milk and Mayor George Moscone. Thousands in San Francisco and beyond mourned Milk's death, with many coming out as gay or marching in his honor. Milk's status as the first openly gay politician inspired many to follow in his footsteps, and he will be remembered as a fighter for all marginalized people.

RENÉE RICHARDS

A lauded tennis player and long-time physician, Dr. Renée Richards served as an anchor for those searching for meaningful LGBTQ+ representation in society. Born in 1934 to Russian-Jewish immigrants in New York and assigned male at birth, Richards had explored gender fluidity as a child by dressing in her sisters' clothing and experiencing discomfort with her body. Richards was raised to be a doctor. Both of her parents were successful doctors, and she followed in their footsteps in her path to Yale, where she became a medical student and a tennis champion. She briefly joined the Navy afterward and won a Navy tennis championship.

Renée Richards takes the court at a tennis match in 1977. Her struggles as a transgender woman paved the way for future trans competitors.

At forty years old, Richards underwent gender-affirming surgeries and began presenting as a woman. After her transition, she moved to Newport Beach, California. Richards attempted to resume playing tennis without exposing her history of presenting as a man. However, after winning the La Jolla Tennis Tournament in 1976, a journalist reported that she had previously competed in men's tournaments.

Controversy erupted, but Richards insisted on competing in whatever event she could. Many players in the women's tournaments she attempted to enter afterward boycotted the events, and the US Tennis Association (USTA) denied her the right to play. She sued the USTA with the goal of playing in the US Open again, as a woman. Though many witnesses came out against her case, openly lesbian tennis star Billie Jean King acted as a witness in her favor. King compellingly argued in the New York Supreme Court that Richards was a woman, and on that basis, she must be able to play. The court ruled in her favor, and while she continued to face opposition, Richards continued playing the sport she loved. She was eventually ranked twentieth in the Women's Tennis Association rankings before retiring from the sport in 1981. In 1983, she published *Second Serve*, an autobiography. As of 2018, Richards lived in a small town in New York and continued to practice medicine.

Jeanne Cordova (*left*) and her partner, Lynn Ballen, lead a demonstration at the East Los Angeles Marriage License Office. They are protesting Proposition 8, a voter-approved ban on same-sex marriage.

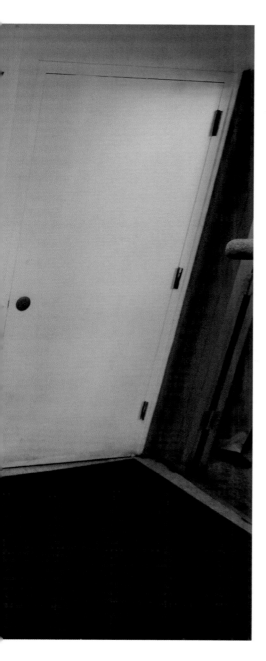

JEANNE CORDOVA

Lesbian activist, lifelong feminist, and accomplished author Jeanne Cordova dedicated her life to furthering gay rights. Born in 1948 in Germany to a Mexican father and an Irish American mother, her family later moved to Los Angeles, where she immersed herself in religious social service. She entered a convent of nuns, the Immaculate Heart of Mary, in 1966. The convent steeped itself in progressive politics, working in the inner cities and protesting the Vietnam War. Cordova embraced this mission of social justice and left the convent in 1968 to pursue a degree in social work at the University of California, Los Angeles.

BISEXUAL ACTIVISM AND ADVOCACY

Bisexual people played a key role in the fight for visibility and advocacy. Groups like the National Bisexual Liberation Group and the Committee of Friends of Bisexuality became anchors in the movement. Bisexual activists Brenda Howard and Donny the Punk are commonly credited with coining the term "Pride" to refer to Christopher Street Liberation Day festivities. Organizers Bill Beasley, Alan Rockway, and Billy Jones sought political representation for LGBTQ+ people.

Bisexuality had also become prominent among many as a means of sexual exploration and liberation. Musicians like Grace Jones are well known for being attracted to both men and women, while David Bowie explored sexual norms in culture and declared himself to be bisexual in 1976. Bisexuality thus became much more visible in the 1970s.

Cordova came out as a lesbian in 1970. As she finished her degree in social work and her thesis on community organizing within the lesbian rights movement, she began organizing for the gay and lesbian community. In 1971, she became the president of the Los Angeles chapter of the Daughters of Bilitis. Cordova saw the need for a newsletter that reflected the growth and progress of the lesbian movement post-Stonewall and spearheaded the new Daughters of Bilitis newspaper, *The Lesbian Tide*. Cordova began editing other local Los Angeles magazines and steeped herself in Democratic politics. She fought alongside other gay politicians, like Harvey Milk, to oppose the Briggs Initiative. Cordova then founded the first convention of the National Lesbian Feminist Organization and became president of the Stonewall Democratic Club.

In the 1980s, Cordova worked to elect LGBTQ+ delegates to the Democratic Party while advocating for victims of AIDS and establishing LGBTQ+ press clubs. She published the Community Yellow Pages, a listing that compiled gay businesses throughout Southern California, before publishing *Kicking the Habit: A Lesbian Nun Story* in 1990 and *Square Peg*, a queer cultural magazine, from 1992 until 1994.

As her life of activism drew to a close, Cordova sponsored lesbian history exhibits throughout Los Angeles and ran a conference for butch lesbians in 2010. In 2011, she released her memoir, *When We Were Outlaws*. She continued to work on behalf of lesbians and LGBTQ+ people throughout the world until she passed away from cancer with her partner by her side in 2016 at sixty-seven years old.

CHAPTER FIVE

SOLIDARITY THROUGH CRISIS

• •

In the 1980s, the LGBTQ+ movement was beginning to break into the mainstream. In addition to politicians and athletes acknowledging their sexuality, artists and musicians began to publicly experiment with sexuality and gender as a new form of cultural subversion. Alfred Kinsey's studies had shown that America was a promiscuous nation that was open to sexual experimentation, and the culture of the 1970s was no different. The conditions were right for the continuation of the expansion of LGBTQ+ visibility in politics and culture.

And then those conditions changed. The AIDS crisis befell the LGBTQ+ community and redefined the goals of the movement. With no help from the government, it was up to the queer community, with their limited knowledge of what was happening, to draw attention to the destruction that many believed only they faced.

VIRGINIA APUZZO

Born into an Italian and Catholic family in New York in 1941, Virginia Apuzzo earned a master's degree in urban education and chose to become a nun. Knowing she was gay from a young age, the GLBTQ Archive records Apuzzo as calling her service "painful but productive," instilling within her a lifelong passion for social justice.

Members of the National Gay Task Force, with whom Virginia Apuzzo worked in pursuit of recognition from the Democratic Party, march at the New York City Gay Pride Parade in 1975.

After reading about the Stonewall riot in a newspaper, she took advantage of the growing movement to come out publicly and take an active role in the movement. She began working with the National Gay Task Force by aiming to secure recognition of LGBTQ+ rights within the Democratic Party's national platform. Apuzzo became the organization's executive director in 1982 after it had been renamed the National Gay and Lesbian Task Force.

AIDS SLOWS GAY PROGRESS

In 1981, doctors discovered clusters of rare and particularly vicious forms of cancer and pneumonia. These illnesses were brought on by an immune system deficiency that appeared in gay populations in San Francisco, Los Angeles, and New York City. Researchers started referring to this mysterious syndrome as GRID, or gay-related immune deficiency. According to the United States Department of Health and Human Services, by year's end, 270 cases of GRID had been recorded among gay men, with 121 of those men having died within months of diagnosis.

Over the next year, more facts became clear. The Center for Disease Control (CDC) discovered the means of transmission for the disease—sexual contact or blood transfusion—and began referring to the disease as acquired immune deficiency syndrome (AIDS).

Eventually, high-profile victims urged the federal government to finally acknowledge the AIDS crisis. These efforts included a communication from Surgeon General C. Everett Koop that encouraged the public to practice safe sex. LGBTQ+ activists came together to further their cause in October 1987 at the Second March on Washington for Lesbian and Gay Rights, which boasted more than two hundred thousand attendees.

The decades that followed the emergence of the crisis marked a time of loss and solidarity within the LGBTQ+ movement and revealed a tragedy that easily could've been greatly reduced with the aid of sustained medical focus.

As executive director of the National Gay Task Force, she worked hard to fight against AIDS. She testified to Congress about the need for federal funding and public recognition. She was appointed vice chair of the New York State AIDS Advisory Board by Governor Mario Cuomo in 1985 and worked to make early AIDS treatments more accessible to all. She climbed the ranks of the federal government, and President Bill Clinton appointed her to the position of associate deputy for the secretary of labor in 1996. She worked with the Clinton administration to ensure those with AIDS would receive adequate disability benefits.

She continued to lecture at various institutions about LGBTQ+ issues and worked in the office of New York governor Eliot Spitzer beginning in 2007. In 2011, she left her post, and she moved to Florida in 2013 to enjoy her retirement.

LARRY KRAMER

Writer and activist Larry Kramer played the role of an incendiary figure in the fight against AIDS. Kramer was born in 1935 and spent his childhood in Connecticut and Maine. He attended Yale but was ostracized due to his homosexuality. Eventually, Kramer found a small community among the campus's glee club, where he gained a passion for playwriting

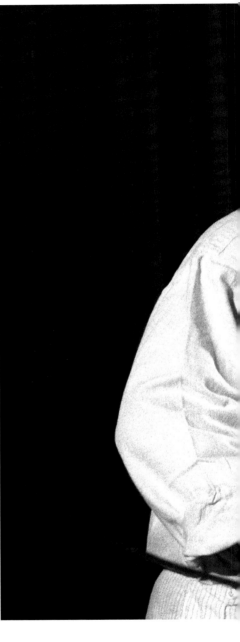

Larry Kramer is speaking at the *Village Voice* AIDS Conference in New York City on June 6, 1987. He is known for advocating for the rights and equal treatment of people with AIDS.

and theatre. In the 1960s, he worked with Columbia Pictures as a screenwriter. This job earned him an Oscar nomination.

After the Stonewall riots, Kramer moved to New York City to be closer to the heart of the movement. He began writing dramas focused on homosexual life. In 1981, Kramer organized a small symposium to discuss the outbreak of Karposi's sarcoma in the New York gay community. This led to the foundation of the Gay Men's Health Crisis (GMHC) in early 1982.

As the disease spread, the numbers of those diagnosed with and killed by AIDS skyrocketed by the thousands. Though gay communities attempted to organize around the goal of dealing with the crisis, the administration of President Reagan refused to openly acknowledge the situation until late into the decade. These developments were immensely frustrating to activists like Kramer, who disagreed with the slower pace of the actions undertaken by his own coalition.

By 1987, ten thousand New Yorkers had been diagnosed with AIDS; half of them had died. At that time, Kramer had long since left the GMHC because he believed that bolder activism was necessary. In March of that year, Kramer became inspired by the slogan SILENCE = DEATH. Community artists created this slogan as a rallying cry against politicians and organizations that refused to acknowledge the crisis. Responding to this call for direct action, Kramer declared in a speech given to attendees at the Lesbian and Gay Community

Center in Manhattan that not acting "is a death wish." This speech inspired more than three hundred activists to form the AIDS Coalition to Unleash Power (ACT UP).

ACT UP began performing radical protests that had the end goal of making treatment for AIDS accessible to all. Within weeks of Kramer's speech, the group's demonstrations created massive upheaval. ACT UP's protests successfully opened access to treatment and drew massive visibility toward the needs of people with AIDS and their caregivers.

Kramer's activism continued well after the formation of ACT UP. In 1988, Kramer tested positive for HIV, the virus that causes AIDS. He continued to write novels about the AIDS crisis and politics even as he battled health crises. This resilience made him a champion for LGBTQ+ people and those who are HIV positive, especially as ACT UP's protests continued throughout the 1990s and into the 2000s.

As of 2018, Kramer was known to spend his days in Manhattan and Connecticut and write about politics and gay culture for various progressive newspapers and blogs.

ESSEX HEMPHILL

Born in 1957, Washington, D.C.-based poet Essex Hemphill is known in the LGBTQ+ community for shining a light on the lives of gay men of color during the AIDS crisis. Hemphill was born in

Chicago, but his family moved to Washington, D.C., shortly after his birth. Like many African American families in Washington, D.C., his family experienced poverty and marginalization, and Hemphill battled those in pursuit of a career in writing.

Hemphill studied journalism briefly at the University of Maryland. After that, he returned to Washington, D.C., to immerse himself in the art scene and to found several groups dedicated to black art and literature. This passion brought him to help produce documentaries on black art, including *Tongues United* (1989), an exploration of the intersections between queerness and being black, and *Black Is... Black Ain't* (1992), which explored the depths of black identity in America.

Hemphill's poetry touched on his identity as a gay black man. He began self-publishing smaller poetry collections, called chapbooks, in 1982. He found critical acclaim with the releases of *Earth Life* in 1985 and *Conditions* in 1986. These poems touched upon the love and loss Hemphill experienced as a member of the black gay community during the AIDS crisis.

While he was hesitant to discuss his own experience with the disease, Hemphill was driven to write about his experiences as a person with AIDS in the early 1990s. Hemphill's 1994 poem "Vital Signs" served as a heartfelt expression of his own battle with the disease and an open admission that his life was coming to an end. Though he died from AIDS-related complications in 1995, Hemphill left behind a legacy of thoughtful exploration of

"RIGGS COULDN'T HAVE LEFT A MORE EFFECTIVE OR CHALLENGING LEGACY"
— Emanuel Levy, VARIETY

Black Filmmakers
Hall of Fame
Best of Festival
1995

SUNDANCE
Filmmakers Trophy
1995

San Francisco
International
Golden Gate Award
1995

"A testament of courage... moving and brilliant"
— Gloria Naylor, AUTHOR

"Brilliant... a powerful, *interesting*, riveting film"
— Alice Walker, AUTHOR

"...a complex and personal exploration"
— David Ansen, NEWSWEEK

"An eloquent tribute... a major contribution to the
exploration of how we develop our identities"
— Emanuel Levy, VARIETY

Black *Is...*
Black *Ain't*

A Film by Controversial Award-Winning Filmmaker
Marlon Riggs

Tara Releasing and California Newsreel Present a Marlon Riggs film
Producer/Director: Marlon Riggs Co-Producer: Nicole Atkinson Co-Director/Editor: Christiane Badgley Co-Editor: Bob Paris
Featuring: Angela Davis, Essex Hemphill, bell hooks, Bill T. Jones, Michele Wallace and Cornel West

TARA
RELEASING

CALIFORNIA
NEWSREEL

Essex Hemphill was involved in the production of *Black Is... Black Ain't*, a 1994 film exploring black identity. Marlon Riggs directed this film but passed away from AIDS complications before it could be released.

parts of the culture that had previously been left unrecorded.

CLEVE JONES

Cleve Jones was born in Indiana in 1954 and grew up feeling isolated due to his sexuality. After reading about the burgeoning gay liberation movement in *Life* magazine, Jones felt instilled with a purpose that would lead him to a career in human rights and activism. He would eventually memorialize the victims of the AIDS crisis and advocate for laborers. He came out as gay to his parents and moved to San Francisco in the early 1970s. There, he participated in the local community and worked alongside Harvey Milk.

Over the next decade, hardship befell Jones. He was distressed by the assassination of Harvey Milk and lost many close to him during the AIDS crisis. In 1985, Jones discovered he was HIV positive. That December, at a memorial service for Milk, he encouraged the thousand-plus attendees to write down the names of those they knew who had died of AIDS. Attendees joined him in taping the many sheets full of names to the walls of a Health and Human Services building in San Francisco. This image brought up the idea for a memorial quilt.

Beginning with a panel dedicated to his best friend, Marvin Feldman, Jones created a quilt that memorialized the names of the thousands of people lost to AIDS. Collecting quilted contributions from

On March 3, 2012, Cleve Jones participated in the American Foundation for Equal Rights and Broadway Impact's reading of *8*, a live chronicle of the trial surrounding Proposition 8.

the community, Jones amassed nearly two thousand panes for the NAMES Project AIDS Memorial Quilt (NAMES Project) before its first public display at the Second March on Washington for Lesbian and Gay Rights in October 1987. The quilt aimed to draw public awareness to the scope of the disease. By then, the deaths of celebrities and children, gay and straight alike, had raised the profile of the crisis. Victims including Hollywood leading man Rock Hudson, musician Freddie Mercury, and Indiana teenager Ryan White had captivated public attention, and all were not only acknowledged, but also memorialized by those who contributed to the quilt.

Jones continued to update the quilt while expanding his own activism. By 2005, the NAMES Project and its quilt memorialized more than forty-four thousand people. Jones began writing books about his experiences, including 2000's *Stitching a Revolution* and the 2016 memoir *When We Rise*, which was adapted as a miniseries for television in 2017. As of 2018, Jones lived in San Francisco, organizing for UNITE HERE, a labor union primarily focused on the hospitality industry.

CHAPTER SIX

THE NEW CIVIL RIGHTS FRONTIER

● ●

B igoted public figures claimed that the AIDS crisis, and any violence endured by LGBTQ+ people, was some form of religious justice upon the community. Tensions caused by this brand of bigotry resulted in the violent deaths of transgender and gay youth, notably Brandon Teena and Matthew Shepard. Their deaths spurred public outcry and drew LGBTQ+ people and their allies together. The reaction to the crisis and the violence of bigotry was that progressives in support of LGBTQ+ people came together.

As the spread of AIDS slowed down in the 1990s, LGBTQ+ people were emboldened by a new sense of public support. They created societies that celebrated LGBTQ+ art and culture, and LGBTQ+ celebrities coming out of the closet became more common. Within the community, new civil rights concerns became the focus, and the fight for self-affirmation grew far beyond the original call for gay and lesbian rights that had rallied the early days of the movement.

An uptick in public support allowed the LGBTQ+ community to coalesce with a renewed focus. Within the LGBTQ+ community, the search for a way forward inspired a fight for more expansive civil rights, including the right to marry and adopt a wider interpretation of queer identities. These avenues of thought drove the movement forward.

DAVID JAY

David Jay, a native of St. Louis, was born in 1982. Throughout the 90s, queer individuals used the internet and online bulletin boards to discuss new forms of sexual and gender identity, such

This is the asexual flag. It is one of many queer flags inspired by Gilbert Baker's original rainbow pride flag. The asexual flag was designed by an AVEN user called standup in 2010.

as gender fluidity, pansexuality, polyamory, and asexuality. Asexuality, in particular, is the subject of Jay's work. Jay, who struggled with his own lack of sexual desire as a teenager, resolved to create a website where individuals who identified as asexual or experienced a lack of sexual attraction could find community and resources. This led to him becoming a leader in one of the new explorations of queerness that occurred in the 2000s.

In 2001, Jay's website, the Asexual Visibility and Education Network (AVEN), went live. The members of AVEN used the new website to explore issues pertaining to asexual advocacy, health, relationships, and identity. Creating AVEN led to Jay becoming a leader in the asexual community. He engaged in interview and lecture circuits on television and at conferences, and he was eventually featured in the 2011 documentary *(A)sexual*.

Jay's success is unique because most online queer culture developed in spaces that were effectively leaderless and community driven. This community-driven culture made AVEN into a product of its membership, with features like user-driven discussion and independently led asexual events thriving on the network's message boards. As of 2018, Jay had worked with the New York City Department of Education and other organizations to promote recognition of asexuality in sexual health curricula.

CHALLENGES OF THE FUTURE

As of 2018, LGBTQ+ people had gained a tremendous amount of ground in the United States. LGBTQ+ individuals had secured major victories in key areas such as political representation, media visibility, marriage rights, and legal recognition.

However, activists feared the ramifications of a potential backlash against these victories. In 2016, eighteen states either passed or introduced laws that would strip transgender people of various rights.

Political upheaval also posed a grave danger to the community and its progress. Activists prepared to fight damaging executive orders from the Trump administration that would take power in 2017 while mitigating the damage caused by the administration's actions regarding immigration and health care.

The movement appears to be taking a more holistic approach. LGBTQ+ activism had finally become a standard part of the greater progressive movement, a platform that worked on behalf of immigrants, women, minorities, and the poor while protecting health care access and the environment. As these concerns impact the lives of LGBTQ+ people, this integration left the movement better prepared to handle the challenges of the future.

JIM OBERGEFELL

Jim Obergefell, a real estate agent, helped realize a longtime dream of gay rights activists, that of marriage recognition for all LGBTQ+ people. Obergefell was born in 1966 to a Catholic family in Cincinnati. In his mid-twenties, he came out to his family as gay. In Cincinnati's social scene, Obergefell met John Arthur at a bar in 1992 and later hit it off with him at a friend's party. Their connection turned into a lifelong relationship, one that lasted for over twenty-two years until Arthur passed away.

Legislation and jurisprudence historically restricted the right of marriage and its protections to heterosexual couples. Activists continued to argue for the right to marry,

Jim Obergefell holds a photo of his late husband John Arthur after the US Supreme Court ruled that same-sex couples have the right to marry in all fifty states in 2015.

and many gay and lesbian couples chose to participate in informal marriages, even if the law would not recognize them. The law wouldn't restrict Obergefell and Arthur from being life partners. Arthur gave Obergefell a symbolic diamond ring.

Several states began to legalize gay marriage, even in the face of the federal government's refusal to grant marriage benefits to gay couples. Obergefell and Arthur's paths became entwined with the fight for marriage rights in this environment. In 2011, Arthur was diagnosed with ALS, or Lou Gehrig's disease. The condition began to impact his ability to move. Arthur wanted to ensure that his partner would be cared for after his death, and after a Supreme Court case banned the federal government's discrimination toward gay couples, Obergefell brought Arthur to Maryland in order to marry him in 2013. Arthur passed away just months after their wedding, and Obergefell filed a lawsuit against Ohio, which had banned gay marriage. He wanted to be listed as the surviving spouse on Arthur's death certificate. This lawsuit climbed its way to the Supreme Court alongside several cases and was renamed *Obergefell v. Hodges*. In a 5–4 decision, the Supreme Court ruled in favor of Obergefell and the other plaintiffs and declared that the Fourteenth Amendment guaranteed lesbian and gay couples the right to marry in every state, and it guaranteed that a state that didn't issue a marriage license must recognize the marriage. Following this landmark decision in 2015, Obergefell continued to participate in activism in celebration of the life of his husband, and he wrote a memoir about his victory, called *Love Wins*, in 2016.

CHASE STRANGIO

As activists celebrated the victory for marriage equality, a new frontier in the fight for LGBTQ+ civil rights emerged. At the forefront was Chase Strangio, an attorney for the American Civil Liberties Union's LGBT & AIDS Project. The topic? Transgender rights.

Strangio, a transgender man, became passionate about social justice work while in college. He was influenced by Dean Spade, a fellow transgender activist who founded the Sylvia Rivera Law Project (SRLP), and worked for the SRLP representing transgender and gender-variant people as part of its Prison Justice Initiative.

As he began his work at the American Civil Liberties Union (ACLU), the United States faced an onslaught of laws that threatened to restrict the rights of transgender people across the country. These proposed laws, such as North Carolina's HB2, attempted to ban transgender people from using the restroom facilities that matched their gender identities. This added to a history of state-sanctioned discrimination and

On September 22, 2016, Chase Strangio, a transgender lawyer for the ACLU, attended the photography exhibition *IDENTITY: Timothy Greenfield-Sanders The List Portraits*, a groundbreaking celebration of marginalized communities.

violence directed toward transgender people. Working on behalf of the ACLU, Strangio fought these laws in court on behalf of transgender clients and earned legal protection and recognition for transgender people. Strangio's clients included Chelsea Manning, a military whistleblower whose status and needs as a transgender woman were not being recognized in prison, and Gavin Grimm, a teenager in Virginia who fought for his right to use the correct restroom in school. In 2018, Grimm continued to work with the ACLU and as an advocate for transgender youth as his case works its way through the legal system.

Outside of court, Strangio founded the Lorena Borjas Community Fund to provide bail assistance for LGBTQ+ immigrants. He wrote several essays published online in support of transgender rights and to draw attention to incidents of discrimination and violence, particularly those against transgender women of color. In an interview with *Vice*, Strangio declared, "We have an obligation as a society to ensure that our systems of health care, of documentation, of public accommodation don't serve to erase [transgender people]."

A PATH FORWARD

The historical issues of the LGBTQ+ community include medical institutionalization, criminalization, employment and housing discrimination, and social ostracization in more intimate environments.

On August 21, 2016, Gavin Grimm posed at his home in Gloucester, Virginia. In August 2017, the Fourth Circuit Court of Appeals in Richmond, Virginia, declined to hear his case, *Gavin Grimm v. Gloucester County School Board*. It was sent back to a lower court.

Removing homosexuality (but not transgenderism) from the *Diagnostic and Statistical Manual of Mental Disorders* was an important event that delegitimized criminalization and involuntary hospitalization. This change also removed the most influential advocate of conversion therapy. But the American Psychiatric Association's action of removing that label only meant freedom in theory because it didn't create a way for acceptance of queer people to become part of mainstream society.

All it takes is one angry parent to chase his or her son or daughter away from home to initiate a path toward homelessness, unemployment, and violence. Sharing an unaccepted identity with one coworker could still mean getting fired and losing financial support. And as the *New York Times* and the Williams Institute revealed in 2015, unchecked police harassment still means that there are not adequate law enforcement protections for queer people. There has been a good deal of progress over the years, but it is still much too easy to lose what little stability LGBTQ+ people have.

But just as queer intervention led to removing homosexuality from the *DSM*, public awareness, media presence, and legislative victories can continue to provide new opportunities and bestow optimism in the hearts of LGBTQ+ people and their allies. Though challenges that threaten to stand in the way of progress continue to arise, the community has never backed down from an opportunity to gain protections. They have always been at the forefront of the fight for their own civil rights and for other marginalized people. The community has offered strong and effective resistance at every turn and faced crises and violence with all the power they have to withstand them. The movement's focus and resolve took new shape with unique issues that presented themselves, and it will likely continue to display such resilience in the future.

TIMELINE

1919 Magnus Hirschfeld opens the world's first LGBTQ+ advocacy and research organization, the Institute for Sex Research in Germany.

1924 Henry Gerber starts the Society for Human Rights, the first LGBTQ+ organization in the United States. Hirschfeld's work was Gerber's inspiration.

1935 Nazis burn Hirschfeld's materials in a bonfire in Germany.

1950 Harry Hay and several other gay men found the Mattachine Society.

1955 The Daughters of Bilitis begins operations.

1964 President Lyndon B. Johnson signs the Civil Rights Act.

1965 President Johnson signs the Voting Rights Act.

1969 The Stonewall riots break out during a police raid in New York City. It is described as the event that galvanized the LGBTQ+ rights movement.

1977 Harvey Milk is elected to the San Francisco Board of Supervisors.

1978 Dan White assassinates Milk and Mayor George Moscone.

1979 Tens of thousands of activists join the March on Washington for Lesbian and Gay Rights.

1981 The first cases of AIDS in the United States appear in San Francisco, Los Angeles, and New York. Within the year, 120 have died.

1987 Over two hundred thousand LGBTQ+ activists attend the second annual March on

Washington for Lesbian and Gay Rights. The AIDS quilt is displayed in public for the first time during this event.

2015 The Supreme Court rules in *Obergefell v. Hodges* that the Fourteenth Amendment of the US Constitution recognizes the right for all couples to marry.

2016 The Supreme Court sends the case of Gavin Grimm, who sued his school seeking recognition under Title IX sex discrimination laws, back to the Fourth Circuit.

2017 In August, the Fourth Circuit sent Grimm's case back to the district court to determine its standing.

GLOSSARY

acquired immune deficiency syndrome (AIDS)
Originally referred to as gay-related immune
deficiency, this syndrome occurs when HIV has
suppressed the immune system to the point where
the body fails to fight off the most basic infections.

asexual A lack of sexual attraction or interest, not
to be confused with being aromantic, or lacking
romantic interest.

bisexual A sexual orientation in which a person
is attracted to men and women or sexes and
genders that don't fit the sex and gender binaries.

blue discharge Named for the blue paper they
were printed on, a kind of military discharge not
considered dishonorable or honorable issued to
homosexual individuals (as well as others) in the
1940s and 1950s that barred recipients from
access to veterans' benefits.

drag queen One who was assigned male at birth
who performs exaggerations of femininity and
womanhood, usually on stage or for personal
pleasure.

gay Also referred to as homosexual, men who feel
a sexual or romantic attraction for other men, or
more generally attraction to people of the same
sex or gender.

gender identity A person's perception of one's
own gender. It may or may not correlate with the
assigned sex at birth.

heterosexuality Sexual and/or romantic attraction toward members of the opposite side of the gender binary that may or may not exclude transgender people.

human immunodeficiency virus (HIV) A viral infection transmitted through contact with a carrier's blood, semen, vaginal fluids, or breast milk that weakens the immune system and causes AIDS.

Kaposi's sarcoma A viral cancer caused by a form of the herpes virus that is characterized by dark, external tumors across the skin, particularly on the nose and mouth.

lesbian A woman who feels a sexual or romantic attraction for other women.

LGBTQ+ An acronym for lesbian, gay, bisexual, transgender, queer, and questioning; it is meant to include all other sexual or gender minorities.

marginalized Neglected or abused by society.

McCarthyism The doctrine of Senator Joseph McCarthy and his allies that insisted homosexuals and Communists were enemies of the United States, leading to the lavender scare and the red scare.

pansexual A sexual orientation posed as an alternative to the term "bisexual" that includes nonbinary gender identities.

progressive A philosophy that advocates for social reform that often works against historically marginalizing and traditional ways of doing things.

queer A word used to describe a person who is a sexual minority and/or transgender person. It was once exclusively used as a slur.

sexology The study of human sexuality from a medical, psychological, and sociological perspective.

sexual inversion A Victorian-era term referring to LGBTQ+ identities, those who were "inverted" from the heterosexual societal norms.

transgender An umbrella of identities that includes people who don't fit into the traditional sex and gender binaries, including transexual and third-gender people.

transsexual An early term referring to transgender individuals who used medical treatments in order to publicly transition to a different gender identity. Now, "transgender" is more commonly used to refer to those who undergo gender-affirming surgeries.

transvestite A term originally used to refer to cross-dressers, it is now considered offensive by many members of the transgender community.

two-spirit A gender identity common in indigenous cultures that can refer to those who embody the spiritual and societal presence of multiple genders, among other identities.

FOR MORE INFORMATION

The Ali Forney Center (AFC)
321 West 125th Street
New York, NY 10027
(212) 206-0574
Website: http://www.aliforneycenter.org
Facebook: @AliForney
Twitter: @AliForneyCenter
The AFC is the largest organization in the United
States dedicated to providing resources, including
housing, job preparedness, and health care
services for LGBTQ+ youth who are homeless.

Canadian Lesbian & Gay Archives
34 Isabella Street
Toronto, ON M4Y 1N1
Canada
(416) 777-2755
Website: http://www.clga.ca
Facebook, Twitter, and Instagram: @CLGArchives
These archives offer a collection of artifacts that
include documents, audio records, pictures, and
other materials from throughout the Canadian
LGBTQ+ movement.

Egale Canada
185 Carlton Street
Toronto, ON M5A 2K7
Canada
(888) 204-7777
Website: http://www.egale.ca

Facebook and Twitter: @EgaleCanada
YouTube: @Egale Canada Human Rights Trust
This organization focuses on increasing equal rights
and access to youth resources and refugee
services. It also offers information specifically
targeted at indigenous two-spirit people.

Equality Forum
1420 Locust Street, Suite 300
Philadelphia, PA 19102
(215) 732-3378
Website: http://www.equalityforum.com
Facebook and Twitter: @EqualityForum
YouTube: @equalityforum
This organization educates others about civil rights
by producing documentaries and planning
international LGBTQ+ civil rights summits.

GLBT Historical Society
989 Market Street
San Francisco, CA 94103
(415) 777-5455
Website: http://www.glbthistory.org
Facebook: @GLBTHistory
YouTube: @GLBT Historical Society
This historical society runs both a comprehensive
historical archive and the GLBT History Museum

Kinsey Institute
Morrison 313
1165 East Third Street
Bloomington, IN 47405

(812) 855-7686
Website: http://www.kinseyinstitute.org
Facebook and Twitter: @kinseyinstitute
YouTube: @Kinsey Institute
This institute studies human sexuality and uses
    artifacts pertaining to sexual expression, along
    with historical archives pertaining to the work of
    Dr. Alfred Kinsey.

National LGBTQ Task Force
1325 Massachusetts Avenue NW, Suite 600
Washington, DC 20005
(202) 393-5177
Website: http://www.thetaskforce.org
Facebook and Twitter: @thetaskforce
This long-standing organization participates in direct
    actions and advocates on behalf of LGBTQ+
    people and offers resources, including advice,
    training, and historical resources.

Sylvia Rivera Law Project
147 West 24th Street, 5th Floor
New York, NY 10011
(212) 337-8550
Website: http://www.srlp.org
Facebook: @SylviaRiveraLawProject
Twitter: @srlp
Youtube: @SylviaRiveraLP
This organization supports self-determining
    a person's gender identity and expression
    regardless of income or race. They also provide
    prisoner advocacy and legal information.

Transgender Law Center
PO Box 70976
Oakland, CA 94612
(510) 587-9696
Website: http://www.transgenderlawcenter.org
Facebook and Twitter: @translawcenter
YouTube: @TransLawCenter
The Transgender Law Center provides legal advice,
   assistance for immigrants and detainees,
   education, and other services at no cost to
   transgender people and their allies.

FOR FURTHER READING

Barker, Meg-John, and Julia Scheele. *Queer: A Graphic History*. London, UK: Icon Books, 2016.

Eaklor, Vicki L. *Queer America: A People's GLBT History of the United States*. New York, NY: The New Press, 2011.

Erickson-Schroth, Laura. *Trans Bodies, Trans Selves: A Resource for the Transgender Community*. New York, NY: Oxford University Press, 2014.

Faderman, Lillian. *The Gay Revolution: The Story of the Struggle*. New York, NY: Simon & Schuster, 2015.

Hollander, Barbara. *Marriage Rights and Gay Rights*. New York, NY: Rosen Publishing, 2015.

Huegel, Kelly. *GLBTQ: The Survival Guide for Gay, Lesbian, Bisexual, Transgender, and Questioning Teens*. Minneapolis, MN: Free Spirit Publishing, 2014.

Jones, Cleve. *When We Rise*. New York, NY: Hachette Books, 2016.

Klein, Rebecca T. *Transgender Rights and Protections*. New York, NY: Rosen Publishing, 2017.

Stryker, Susan. *Transgender History*. Berkeley, CA: Seal Press, 2017.

Thompson, Tamara. *Transgender People* (At Issue). New York, NY: Greenhaven Publishing, 2015.

BIBLIOGRAPHY

Bullough, Vern L. *Before Stonewall: Activists for Gay and Lesbian Rights in Historical Context*. Binghamton, NY: Harrington Park Press, 2002.

Carter, David. *Stonewall: The Riots that Sparked the Gay Revolution*. New York, NY: St. Martin's Press, 2013.

Cenziper, Debbie, and James Obergefell. *Love Wins*. New York, NY: Affirm Press, 2016.

Chan, Vanessa. "Urban Profile: David Jay, Asexual—Sexless and Satisfied." Urban Profile, December 18, 2012. http://untappedcities .com/2012/12/18/urban-profile-david-jay -asexual-sexless-and-satisfied.

Cleves, Rachel Hope. *Charity & Sylvia: A Same-Sex Marriage in Early America*. New York, NY: Oxford University Press, 2014.

Cox, David. "The Danish Girl and the Sexologist: A Story of Sexual Pioneers." *The Guardian*, January 13, 2016. https://www.theguardian .com/science/blog/2016/jan/13/magnus -hirschfeld-groundbreaking-sexologist-the-danish -girl-lili-elbe.

Gerber/Hart Library and Archives. "Meet Henry and Pearl..." Retrieved March 12, 2017. http://www .gerberhart.org/meet-henry-and-pearl.

Gross, Terry. "LGBTQ Activist Cleve Jones: 'I'm Well Aware How Fragile Life Is'." NPR, November 29, 2016. http://www.npr.org/2016/11/29 /503724044/lgbtq-activist-cleve-jones-im-well -aware-how-fragile-life-is.

Hainey, Michael. "The Woman Who Paved the Way for Men to Become Women." *GQ*, May 26, 2015. http://www.gq.com/story/renee-richards -interview?currentPage=1.

JeanneCordova.com. "A Tsunami of a Life." Retrieved April 8, 2017. http://jeannecordova .com/index.php?option=com_content&view =article&id=50&Itemid=57.

Kaplan, Sarah. "A Poet Who Spoke to the Black Gay Experience, and a Quest to Make Him Heard." *Washington Post*, August 3, 2014. https://www.washingtonpost.com /lifestyle/style/a-poet-who-spoke-to-the-black -gay-experience-and-a-quest-to-make-him-heard /2014/08/03/91307a2a-1ac6-11e4-9e3b -7f2f110c6265_story.html?utm_term =.ea0c6a42b998.

King, Jamilah. "Meet the Trans Women of Color Who Helped Put Stonewall on the Map." Mic, June 25, 2015. https://mic.com/articles /121256/meet-marsha-p-johnson-and-sylvia -rivera-transgender-stonewall-veterans #.IYqOlbhzg.

NPR. "American Lives: James Baldwin, 'Lifting the Veil.'" NPR, *Morning Edition,* August 19, 2010. http://www.npr.org/templates/story/story.php ?storyId=129281259.

Reyes, Raul A. "A Forgotten Latina Trailblazer: LGBT Activist Sylvia Rivera." NBC News, October 6, 2015. http://www.nbcnews.com/news /latino/forgotten-latina-trailblazer-lgbt-activist -sylvia-rivera-n438586.

Roscoe, Will. *The Zuni Man-Woman*. Albuquerque, NM: University of New Mexico Press, 1991.

Ryanne, Sadie. "Proof Emma Goldman Would Support Trans Liberation." Queerly Mad, March 25, 2012. https://queerlymad.com/2012/03/25/proof-emma-goldman-would-be-a-tranarchist.

Sonnenberg, Zoë. "Daughers of Bilitis." FoundSF. Retrieved April 8, 2017. http://www.foundsf.org/index.php?title=Daughters_of_Bilitis.

Summers, Claude J. "Sagarin, Edward (Donald Webster Cory) (1913-1986)." Retrieved April 8, 2017. http://www.glbtqarchive.com/ssh/sagarin_e_S.pdf.

Tourjee, Diana. "The Trans Lawyer Fighting to Keep His Community Alive." *Vice*, September 27, 2016. https://broadly.vice.com/en_us/article/chase-strangio-the-trans-lawyer-fighting-to-keep-his-community-alive.

INDEX

ABOUT THE AUTHOR

Ellen McGrody is an author and activist dedicated to shining a spotlight on the lives of transgender people. She founded Run for Our Rights, an annual gaming marathon benefiting the Transgender Law Center, and Good Lil' Trans Girl, a parody blog that tackles transmisogyny through humor. Her writing credits include *Coping with Gender Dysphoria*, and she has been featured at TRANSform Tech, Lost Levels, GaymerX, and the Queerness and Games Conference. McGrody lives with her fiancée and cat in Oakland, California.

PHOTO CREDITS

Cover (top) Leo Mason/Popperfoto/Getty Images; cover (bottom) Ulf Andersen/Hulton Archive/Getty Images; pp. 6–7 esfera/Shutterstock.com; p. 7 (inset) Robert Clay/Alamy Stock Photo; p. 11 Pictorial Press Ltd/Alamy Stock Photo; p. 15 ullstein bild/Getty Images; pp. 16–17 Keystone-France/Gamma-Keystone/Getty Images; p. 20 Chronicle/Alamy Stock Photo; p. 25 Frank Scherschel/The LIFE Picture Collection/Getty Images; pp. 28–29, 58–59, 60–61 Bettmann/Getty Images; p. 31 H.S. Photos/Alamy Stock Photo; pp. 34–35 Rachel Ritchie/KRT/Newscom; pp. 38–39, 52–53, 54–55 © AP Images; p. 43 Robert Abbott Sengstacke/Archive Photos/Getty Images; pp. 48–49 Drew Angerer/Getty Images; p. 64 Getty Images; pp. 66–67 Robert Hanashiro-Pool/Getty Images; p. 71 Archive Photos/Getty Images; pp. 74–75 Catherine McGann/Hulton Archive/Getty Images; p. 79 John D. Kisch/Separate Cinema Archive/Moviepix/Getty Images; p. 81 Michael Buckner/Getty Images; pp. 84–85 –1001–/iStock/Thinkstock; pp. 88–89 Alex Wong/Getty Images; p. 92 Chris Weeks/Getty Images; p. 94 The Washington Post/Getty Images.

Design: Michael Moy; Layout: Nicole Russo-Duca;
Editor: Bernadette Davis; Photo Research: Karen Huang